This book belongs to

_____

Copyright © 2021 by Humor Heals Us. All rights reserved. No part of this book may be reproduced in any form without permission in writing from the publisher. Please send questions and requests to humorhealsus@gmail.com Printed and bound in the USA. 978-1-63731-075-5 Humorhealsus.com

Abe the Farting Ape's April Fool's Day

By Humor Heals Us

Joke Jungle

When we're playing hide and seek, sometimes I let it out in the jungle. Letting out gas is not a good way to hide because if they don't find me by way of smell, they find me by the noises I make. Joke's on me!

Clever Clown

Have you ever been eating in the cafeteria with friends and then suddenly you let one rip? But no one can tell it's you because it was silent?

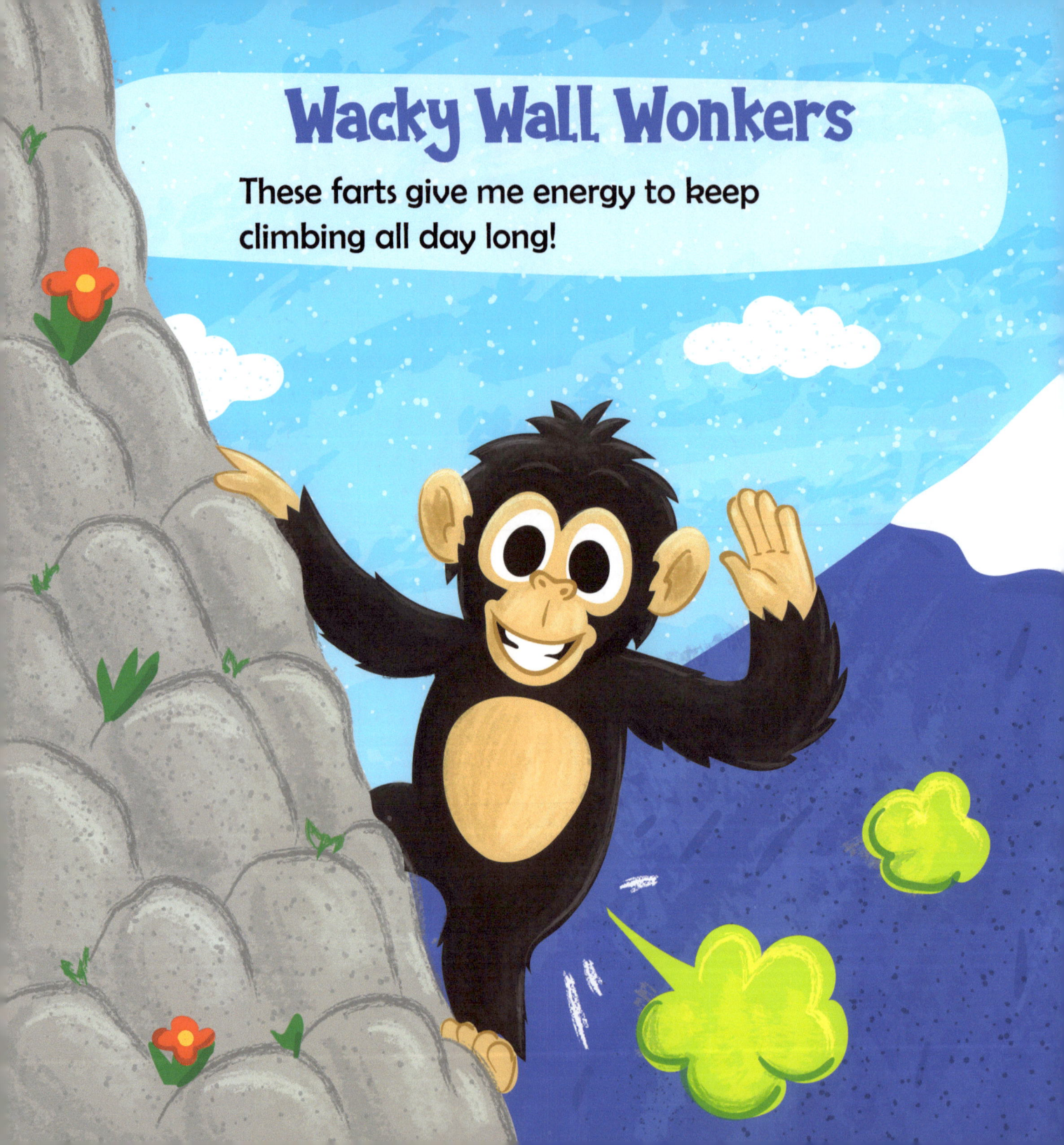

Wacky Wall Wonkers

These farts give me energy to keep climbing all day long!

LOL Surprise!

The best presents are the ones you're not expecting...

Silent safari

It doesn't happen often, but when it does, it brings out the wildest animals in the safari. Since they are hunting for meat, the smells are irresistible!

Natural Joker Instinct

All right. I admit my farts do smell, but isn't it better to laugh at myself than to be embarrassed by this natural instinct?

Fool's Gold

Have you ever had this feeling that you needed to do #2? And come to find out - it was **fool's gold** and not the real thing.

Nice Toots

Pranks and jokes on April fool's Day can be super funny. Just be sure they're not mean because that wouldn't be so fun for everyone.

See you next time in our next book - My Pooting Papa.

Follow us on FB and IG @humorhealsus To vote on new title names and freebies, visit us at humorhealsus.com for more information.

 @humorhealsus  @humorhealsus

www.ingramcontent.com/pod-product-compliance
Lightning Source LLC
Chambersburg PA
CBHW041524070526
44585CB00002B/66